JIMMY LEE DID IT
BY PAT CUMMINGS

Here's all the great literature in this grade level of *Celebrate Reading!*

The Tub People

ILLUSTRATIONS RICHARD EGIELSKI

AVON CAMELOT

AMELIA BEDELIA HELPS OUT
BY PEGGY PARISH
Pictures by Lynn Sweat

BOOK A

Once Upon a Hippo

Ways of Telling Stories

Hot Hippo
by Mwenye Hadithi
Illustrations by
Adrienne Kennaway
✳ KATE GREENAWAY
AUTHOR/ILLUSTRATOR MEDAL

Rosa and Blanca
retold by Joe Hayes
Illustrations by José Ortega

Three Up a Tree
by James Marshall
✳ CHILDREN'S CHOICE AUTHOR

**There's a Hole
in the Bucket**
Illustrations by
Nadine Bernard Westcott

Two Chinese Rhymes
Illustrations by Ed Young

Jimmy Lee Did It
by Pat Cummings
✳ CORETTA SCOTT KING
AWARD ILLUSTRATOR

Featured Poets

Beatrice Schenk de Regniers
Ed Young

The Big Blank Piece of Paper

Artists at Work

Regina's Big Mistake
by Marissa Moss
* NOTABLE SOCIAL STUDIES TRADE BOOK
* PARENTS MAGAZINE BEST KIDS' BOOK

Totem Pole Boy
by Deborah H. DeFord

Emma's Dragon Hunt
by Catherine Stock
* READING RAINBOW SELECTION

Giants
by Syd Hoff
* NY TIMES BOOK REVIEW OUTSTANDING
CHILDREN'S BOOK AUTHOR

The Chicken and the Egg
by Judith Martin

Frog and Toad Are Friends
from the book by Arnold Lobel
* CALDECOTT HONOR BOOK

The Book of Pigericks
from the collection by
Arnold Lobel
* CHILDREN'S CHOICE
* READING RAINBOW SELECTION

Eddy B, Pigboy
by Olivier Dunrea
* LIBRARY OF CONGRESS BOOKS
FOR CHILDREN

Pete Pats Pigs
by Dr. Seuss

Fifty Simple Things Kids
Can Do to Save the Earth
from the book by the
EarthWorks Group

Featured Poets

Dr. Seuss
Robert Louis Stevenson
Aileen Fisher
Tomie dePaola
Alonzo Lopez

BOOK C

You Be the Bread and I'll Be the Cheese

Showing How We Care

Molly the Brave and Me
by Jane O'Connor
Illustrations by
Sheila Hamanaka

The Relatives Came
by Cynthia Rylant
Illustrations by
Stephen Gammell
✳ NEWBERY MEDAL HONOR BOOK
✳ NEW YORK TIMES BEST ILLUSTRATED
CHILDREN'S BOOK

Helping Out
by George Ancona
✳ READING RAINBOW SELECTION

Amelia Bedelia Helps Out
by Peggy Parish
✳ CHILDREN'S CHOICE AUTHOR

The Mother's Day Sandwich
by Jillian Wynot
Illustrations by Maxie Chambliss
✳ CHILDREN'S CHOICE ILLUSTRATOR

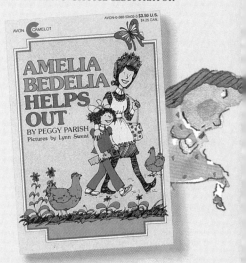

**Come Quick!:
A Play for April Fools' Day**
by Sue Alexander

Hello, Amigos!
by Tricia Brown

Featured Poets

Mary Ann Hoberman
Charlotte Pomerantz

BOOK D

Why Does Water Wiggle?

Learning About the World

Big Goof and Little Goof
from the book by
Joanna and Philip Cole
✱ ALA NOTABLE CHILDREN'S
BOOK AUTHOR
✱ CHILDREN'S CHOICE AUTHOR

Dr. Zed's Science Surprises
from the book by
Gordon Penrose

Tomás and the Library Lady
by Pat Mora

**My Dog and the
Green Sock Mystery**
by David Adler
Illustrations by
Dick Gackenbach
✱ CCBC CHOICE AUTHOR

Fables from Around the World
retold by Janet Stevens,
Nancy Ross Ryan, and
Julius Lester

Animals Learning
from the book by Jane Burton

Buffy's Orange Leash
by Stephen Golder and
Lise Memling

Featured Poets

Jack Prelutsky
Lessie Jones Little

BOOK E

How to Talk to Bears
And Other Tips for Success

Higher on the Door
by James Stevenson
❋ PARENTS' CHOICE
❋ REDBOOK CHILDREN'S BOOK AWARD

Soccer Sam
by Jean Marzollo
Illustrations by Chris Hopkins
❋ READING RAINBOW SELECTION

Featured Poet

Eloise Greenfield

Nessa's Fish
by Nancy Luenn
Illustrations by Neil Waldman
❋ NOTABLE SOCIAL STUDIES TRADE BOOK
❋ ALA NOTABLE CHILDREN'S BOOK

With the Wind
by Liz Damrell
Illustrations by
Stephen Marchesi

Minnie the Mambo Mosquito
by Carmen Tafolla
Illustrations by Ruben Ramos

Gino Badino
by Diana Engel

Oh No, It's Waylon's Birthday!
from the book by
James Stevenson
❋ CHILDREN'S CHOICE

BOOK F

Bathtub Voyages

Tales of Adventure

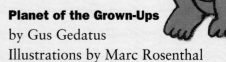

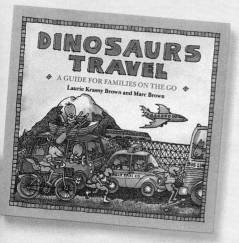

Planet of the Grown-Ups
by Gus Gedatus
Illustrations by Marc Rosenthal

The Tub People
by Pam Conrad
Illustrations by Richard Egielski
❋ CHILDREN'S CHOICE
❋ ALA NOTABLE CHILDREN'S BOOK
❋ PARENTS' CHOICE

My Dog Is Lost!
by Ezra Jack Keats
and Pat Cherr
❋ CALDECOTT MEDAL ILLUSTRATOR

The Lost Lake
by Allen Say
❋ OUTSTANDING SCIENCE TRADE BOOK
❋ CALDECOTT MEDAL ILLUSTRATOR

Dinosaurs Travel:
A Guide for Families on the Go
from the book by
Laurie Krasny Brown
and Marc Brown
❋ TEACHERS' CHOICE AUTHOR
AND ILLUSTRATOR

Dinosaurs, Dragonflies, and
Diamonds: All About Natural
History Museums
by Gail Gibbons
❋ OUTSTANDING SCIENCE TRADE BOOK

Featured Poets

John Ciardi
Sioux Indian Songs

Celebrate Reading!
Trade Book Library

Frog and Toad Together
by Arnold Lobel
❋ NEWBERY MEDAL HONOR BOOK
❋ ALA NOTABLE CHILDREN'S BOOK
❋ *SCHOOL LIBRARY JOURNAL* BEST BOOK
❋ READING RAINBOW SELECTION
❋ LIBRARY OF CONGRESS
   CHILDREN'S BOOK

**The Lady with the
Alligator Purse**
by Nadine Bernard Westcott
❋ CHILDREN'S CHOICE

**Henry and Mudge in
Puddle Trouble**
by Cynthia Rylant
❋ GARDEN STATE CHILDREN'S
   BOOK AWARD

Tyrannosaurus Was a Beast
by Jack Prelutsky
❋ OUTSTANDING SCIENCE TRADE BOOK

A Chair for My Mother
by Vera Williams
❋ CALDECOTT MEDAL HONOR BOOK
❋ ALA NOTABLE CHILDREN'S BOOK
❋ READING RAINBOW SELECTION
❋ BOSTON GLOBE-HORN BOOK AWARD

Paul Bunyan
by Steven Kellogg
❋ READING RAINBOW SELECTION

Big & Little Book Library

Rockabye Crocodile
by Jose Aruego and
Ariane Dewey

Putting on a Play
by Caroline Feller Bauer
Illustrations by Cyd Moore
❋ CHRISTOPHER AWARD AUTHOR

We Are Best Friends
by Aliki
❋ CHILDREN'S CHOICE AUTHOR

Fables from Around the World
retold by Lily Toy Hong,
Carmen Tafolla, Tom Paxton,
Joseph Bruchac, and
Nancy Ross Ryan

Wings: A Tale of Two Chickens
by James Marshall
❋ CHILDREN'S CHOICE AUTHOR
❋ PARENTS' CHOICE AUTHOR
❋ ALA NOTABLE BOOK AUTHOR

Is There Life in Outer Space?
by Franklyn M. Branley
Illustrations by Don Madden
❋ READING RAINBOW BOOK

HOW TO TALK
TO BEARS

AND OTHER TIPS FOR SUCCESS

Titles in This Set

Once Upon a Hippo
The Big Blank Piece of Paper
You Be the Bread and I'll Be the Cheese
Why Does Water Wiggle?
How to Talk to Bears
Bathtub Voyages

About the Cover Artist
David McPhail lives in Newburyport, Massachusetts,
in the house where he grew up. He has four children
and three stepchildren, and he likes to ride his bike.

ISBN 0-673-81134-4

1997
Scott, Foresman and Company, Glenview, Illinois
All Rights Reserved.
Printed in the United States of America.

Acknowledgments appear on page 144.

2345678910DQ010099989796

HOW TO TALK TO BEARS

AND OTHER TIPS FOR SUCCESS

ScottForesman

A Division of HarperCollins*Publishers*

TABLE OF CONTENTS

What Can I Do?

Soccer Sam   6
Realistic fiction by Jean Marzollo
Illustrations by Chris Hopkins

Nessa's Fish   28
Realistic fiction by Nancy Luenn
Illustrations by Neil Waldman

"To Catch a Fish"   46
Poem by Eloise Greenfield
Illustrations by Amos Ferguson

With the Wind   48
Poem by Liz Damrell
Illustrations by Stephen Marchesi

Animal Antics
Genre Study

Minnie the Mambo Mosquito   64
Animal fantasy by Carmen Tafolla
Illustrations by Ruben Ramos

A Word from the Author   72
Narrative nonfiction by Carmen Tafolla

Gino Badino   76
Animal fantasy by Diana Engel

James Stevenson: Full of Laughs
Author Study

"Slippery Ice"   98
from *Oh No, It's Waylon's Birthday!*
Animal fantasy by James Stevenson

READ ALONG

Higher on the Door   110
Autobiography by James Stevenson

A Word from the Author/Illustrator   132
Narrative nonfiction by James Stevenson

Student Resources

Books to Enjoy   136
Literary Terms   138
Glossary   140

6

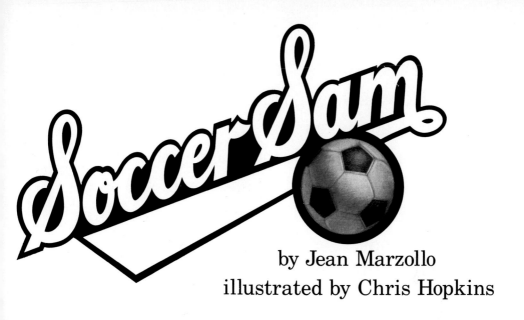

Soccer Sam

by Jean Marzollo
illustrated by Chris Hopkins

The plane from Mexico was landing. Sam stood at the airport window and watched. He was going to meet his cousin Marco for the first time.

Soon a boy Sam's size came through the door. Sam's mother hugged him. "Marco, this is Sam," she said slowly. "Sam, this is Marco."

"Hi," said Sam. Suddenly he felt shy.

"¡Hola!" said Marco softly.

In the car Marco was very quiet. So was Sam.

"We are happy you have come to live with us for a year," said Sam's mother.

"Sí," said Marco. But he didn't look happy. He just looked out the window.

7

"You like sports?" asked Sam. Sam loved sports. He was very good at them too.

Marco shrugged.

"He doesn't speak much English," said Sam's mother. When they got home, she said, "Take Marco out to play, Sam. Introduce him to your friends."

"What if he doesn't understand what we say?" asked Sam.

"Speak slowly," said his mom. "He'll learn."

Sam and Marco went outside. At the end of the street, kids were shooting baskets. Sam's friend Rosie tossed him the ball. Sam aimed and fired. The ball sailed through the rim.

"This is my cousin Marco," Sam said. He tried to talk slowly, but it was hard. "Marco, this is Billy, Chris, Rosie, Tommy, and Freddy."

Billy shot Marco the ball. Marco caught it on his head and bounced it up and down like a seal. Everyone started to laugh at him. Sam's face got hot. He grabbed the ball and made another basket.

Chris caught the ball under the net. He threw it to Marco.

This time Marco caught the ball on his knee and bounced it up and down.

Again everyone laughed at him.

Sam felt awful. "Let's go home," he told Marco.

The next day Sam and Marco went to school together. At recess they played kickball. When the ball came to Marco, he stopped it with his feet.

"Don't you ever use your arms?" asked Freddy. But Marco didn't understand. The next time the ball came to him, he stopped it with his feet again.

Back home Sam tried to explain the rules of sports to Marco.

"Hold the ball in your hands," said Sam. "When you play basketball, bounce the ball as you run. It's called dribbling."

But Marco just looked at Sam. He didn't understand English. He couldn't even say Sam's name right. He said Sammee.

The next day after school, Sam didn't want to go outside. He didn't want to play ball. He was afraid his friends would make fun of Marco.

"Why don't you draw?" Sam's mother asked. So Sam got out his crayons. He drew a picture of a basketball player. Marco drew a picture of his mother and father.

Sam's mother looked at the pictures. "You know what I think?" she said. "I think Marco's homesick. Let's take him to the mall to cheer him up."

At the mall Sam's mother bought Marco a Giants shirt. But it didn't make Marco happy. He didn't know who the Giants were.

"Let's try some video games," said Sam. "Watch. I'll show you how to play." Sam played Pac-Man and got a very high score. "Now you go," he said to Marco. "Don't worry if you don't get a good score at first."

Marco played Pac-Man and got a better score than Sam. He laughed. "In Mexico is Pac-Man also," he said. Marco beat Sam at every game in the arcade.

They walked farther down the mall, looking at stores. When they came to the sports store, Sam stopped to look at footballs. But Marco wasn't interested in footballs. He ran over to a display of black and white balls in boxes. Suddenly he was grinning from ear to ear.

"Why didn't I think of this before?" said Sam's mom. "Most kids in Mexico play soccer."

"Soccer? Nobody plays that around here," said Sam.

"Well, maybe they will now," said his mother with a smile.

Back home Marco took his new ball
outside. He bounced it on his head. He kicked
it around with his feet.

Chris and Billy came over. Marco
kicked the ball to Chris. Chris caught it
with his hands.

"No hands," said Marco.

He kicked the ball to Billy. Billy caught
it with his hands too.

"No hands!" yelled Marco. "Head! Head!"
He bounced the ball on his head.

Then Marco kicked the ball to Sam. Sam let the ball fall on his head.

"¡Bien!" cried Marco. "¡Bien, Sammee!"

Sam laughed. He kicked the ball back to Marco, who kicked it to Billy. Billy bounced it back to Sam with his head.

"¡Bien, Billy!" said Marco. Then he kicked the ball to Chris.

Chris caught it on his head and bounced it to Billy. Billy caught it on his head and bounced it to Sam.

"This is awesome!" said Sam.

"Let's bring the ball to school tomorrow," said Chris.

"We'll show the other kids how to play," said Billy.

"¡Qué bien!" said Marco. "Good!"

The next day at recess Marco showed the other second graders how to play soccer. They stood in a circle and passed the ball around with their heads. Once Sam caught the ball with his hands.

"No hands!" yelled Marco.

The next time someone caught the ball with his hands, everyone yelled, "NO HANDS!" It was fun.

Then Marco told them to pass the ball with their feet. Once Chris picked up the ball with his hands. "NO HANDS!" everyone shouted.

The third graders came by and laughed. "No hands?" they said. "What a weird game."

Some of the second graders felt stupid. They didn't like to be teased by third graders.

"Forget it," said Sam. "I've got a plan. Let's practice all week. Then we'll challenge the third graders to a game. They beat us in football. They beat us in basketball. And they beat us in baseball. But they won't beat us in soccer, will they?"

The second graders liked the plan. They practiced all week. Sam practiced most of all.

On Friday morning Sam went up to the third graders in the playground. "If you think you're so hot," he said, "play soccer with us at lunch. Then we'll see who's really hot."

The third graders took the challenge. Then everyone went back to class. It was hard to study.

Billy said 5 plus 4 was 8.

Chris dropped his notebook on the floor and all his papers fell out.

Marco was so excited he forgot the capital of the United States. He said it was Dallas, Texas.

Sam was so excited, he could hardly write his spelling words.

Finally it was lunchtime. Everyone ate quickly and rushed outside.

The second and third graders met on the field. Sam marked the goals with jackets. Billy went over the rules. "Only the goalie can catch the ball," he said. "To score you have to kick the ball past the goalie and into the place marked by jackets."

The game began. Marco passed the ball to Chris. Chris started to dribble the ball up the field. One of the third graders ran in front of him. Chris passed the ball to Sam.

Sam kicked the ball hard but missed.
The ball sat on the field. A third grader ran
up and kicked it way down the field.

What a kick! The third graders were really big and strong. Another third grader kicked the ball into the third graders' goal. The score was 1–0. The third graders were ahead.

Sam looked worried.

"No importa," said Marco. He dribbled the ball to the opposite goal all by himself. Third graders tried to get the ball away from Marco, but he zigzagged around them. Two of the third graders fell down trying to catch Marco.

"Go, Marco baby!" yelled Billy.

Marco kicked the ball at the second graders' goal. It went in! Now the score was a 1–1 tie.

"Hooray!" shouted Sam.

The third graders had the ball now. One of them kicked it halfway down the field. Another one dribbled it to the third-grade goal. He took aim and fired. Tommy, who was goalie for the second graders, caught the ball.

"Hooray!" shouted Sam again. He knew it was all right for Tommy to catch the ball. In soccer, goalies are the only players who can do that.

Tommy threw the ball to Sam. Sam passed it to Marco. Marco ran it down to the other end and passed it back to Sam. Sam gave it a good hard kick. The ball sailed over the goalie's head. Now the score was 2–1.

The third graders weren't used to losing. They began to make mistakes. They caught the ball with their hands. Every time they did, the second graders shouted, "NO HANDS!"

The second graders started scoring like crazy. Bam! Chris got a goal. Slam! He got another one. Wham! Wham! Wham! Billy got one goal, and Rosie got two.

But Sam and Marco were the team stars. They ran circles around the third graders. They scored six goals each. When lunchtime was over, the score was 19–1.

"A wipe-out!" said Sam.

The third graders were good losers. They all shook hands with the second graders. Then they asked Marco if he would teach them how to play better.

"Sí," said Marco. "Soccer Sammee teach you too."

25

Everybody laughed. "Soccer Sammee!" they shouted. "Soccer Sammee!"

And that's how Sam got his nickname. At first he wasn't sure if he liked it or not.

"Is bueno?" asked Marco. "You like new name?"

Sam looked at his cousin. He knew that anything Marco gave him, he would like. "Sí," said Sam. "I like. Gracias."

Thinking ABOUT IT

1. ¡Hola! Put yourself in Marco's shoes. What would be the most difficult part of visiting a different country? Why?

2. A 19–1 wipe-out! The second graders won the game. Why do you think they won?

3. The third graders want to play another soccer game against the second graders in a week. Who do you think will win? Why do you think so?

Another Book About Winning

In *Ronald Morgan Goes to Bat* by Patricia Reilly Giff, Ronald Morgan can't play baseball very well. But he has another talent that could help his team win.

NESSA'S FISH

by Nancy Luenn
illustrated by Neil Waldman

At autumn camp, Nessa and her grandmother walked inland half a day to fish in the stony lake.

They jigged for fish all afternoon and evening. They caught more than they could carry home. They caught enough to feed everyone in camp.

Nessa and her grandmother stacked up the fish. They piled stones over them to keep away the foxes. Then, tired out, they fell asleep.

During the night, her grandmother was very sick from something she had eaten. Morning came and she needed to rest until she felt better.

Nessa watched over her grandmother. She brought her fresh water from the stony lake. She sat beside her while the sun rose slowly in the sky.

At noon a fox came and sniffed at the stones that covered the fish.

"Go away."

Her grandmother's voice was only a whisper. The fox didn't listen.

Nessa flapped her arms and shouted, "Go away!"

The fox dashed off across the tundra.

The sun rolled a little lower in the sky. A pack of wolves loped toward them and grinned at the stones that covered the fish.

"Do wolves eat fish?" asked Nessa, but her grandmother was asleep. Nessa thought she knew what to do. Her grandfather had told her how to talk to wolves.

She made herself as tall as she could. She made her hands into ears, tipped them forward, and stared straight into the lead wolf's yellow eyes.

"Go away," she growled. "These are *our* fish."

The wolf lowered his tail and grinned apologies at Nessa. He led his pack away across the tundra.

The sun sank behind the hills. Shadows reached across the land. Out of the shadows came a huge, brown bear. Nessa shivered. Bears ate almost *anything.* She wanted to run, but her mother had told her never to run from bears. She waved her fishing pole at the bear and shouted, "Go away!"

The bear stood up on its hind legs and stared. Nessa looked at its long, sharp claws. Would it eat all the fish? Would it eat her grandmother? Would it eat her, too? She tried to remember how to talk to bears.

Her father had told her that a bear would go away if you made it feel foolish. Nessa began to sing.

Skinny old bear
Fur falling out
Big ugly paws
And long pointy snout!

The bear looked surprised. It took one step backward, then another. Nessa sang again.

Skinny old bear
Foolish thing
You can't sing
You can't sing!

The bear's long face did look foolish. It *couldn't* sing. It turned around and shuffled off across the tundra.

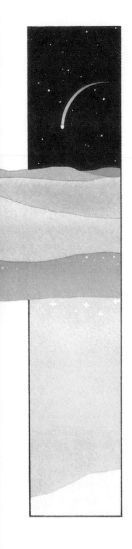

Nessa was very tired. Her
grandmother was sleeping. She tried
to stay awake, for she had to watch
over her.

But no one had told her how to
make sleep go away.

The moon rose over the tundra.
It shone down on Nessa, fast asleep,
curled up beside her grandmother.
It shone on the stones that covered
the fish.

The moon watched over them all
until a noise woke Nessa.

She grabbed her fishing pole and sat
up very tall. Was it the fox? Was it the
wolves? Was it the *bear?*

It was her grandfather! With him were her mother and father and all of the dogs. They had come to look for Nessa and her grandmother.

Everyone hugged her. The dogs waved their tails. Her grandmother woke up and smiled.

Nessa felt good. She had watched over her grandmother. And she had guarded the fish that would feed everyone in camp.

When morning came again, her grandmother felt better. They put the fish in skin bags for the dogs to carry. Then they all walked homeward half a day to autumn camp.

THINKING ABOUT IT

1. Grandmother was sick, so Nessa had to take care of her. How do you take care of someone else? Could you give Nessa any advice?

2. Would Nessa make a good guide for someone visiting the Arctic? Why or why not?

3. Bears are dangerous! What if Nessa's song hadn't made the bear go away? What else could she have done? Give her a plan.

Another Book About Ice Fishing
Eva, a young Inuit girl, walks *under* the ice for the very first time in *Very Last First Time* by Jan Andrews.

To Catch a Fish

by Eloise Greenfield
illustrated by Amos Ferguson

It takes more than a wish
to catch a fish
you take the hook
you add the bait
you concentrate
and then you wait
you wait   you wait
but not a bite
the fish don't have
an appetite
so tell them what
good bait you've got
and how your bait
can hit the spot
this works a whole
lot better than
a wish
if you really
want to catch
a fish

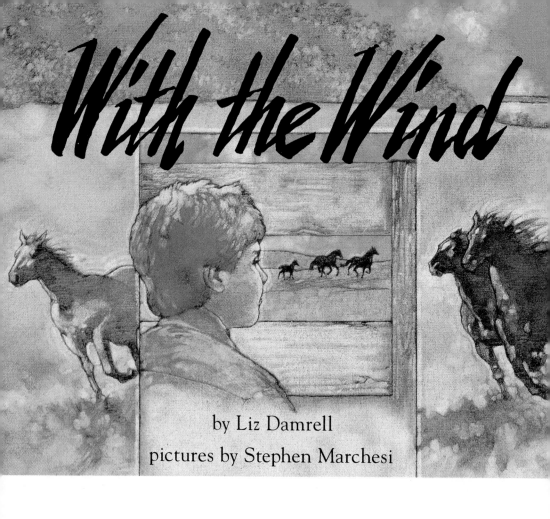

With the Wind

by Liz Damrell

pictures by Stephen Marchesi

He comes out to the field
to see them run.

He puts his hand through the fence—
Carefully—

To touch their soft, strong faces.

When it's time for him to ride
He closes his eyes
To feel the strength beneath him.

When he moves he's alive
To the sounds
The sights
The smells
The feel of the horse's life—

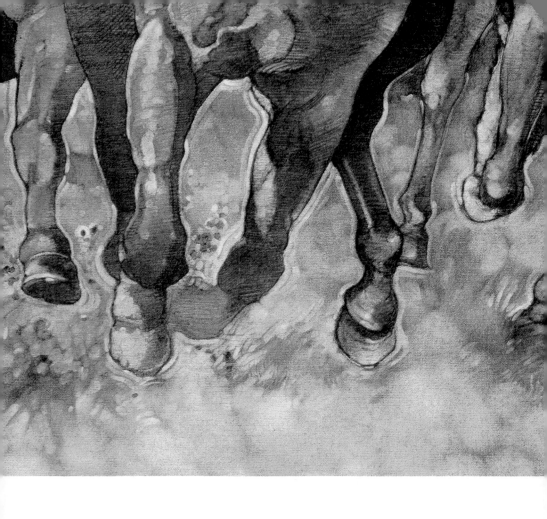

The Freedom.

Through the legs and the hooves
Of the horse

He can feel
The earth move
Away.

As the wind whips his hair
He sits in the air.

He rides through the field—

Among the horses
Among the riders

Alone with the joy—
Alone—

Feeling the power—
A Rider of Horses!

On the ground

People wait for him
To return.

He waves—
As if from a far distance—

Wanting them to know
What
A Rider of Horses
Feels—

Alone—
On top of the creature,
He knows.

Together,
With the riders—
He knows.

Going away—

What he has
Felt
Strengthening him

Beyond

Beyond the field

Where the Horses Run.

Thinking About It

1. Riding horseback with the wind in his hair, the boy feels freedom and power. What do you do that makes you feel this way? Explain.

2. Be the boy in the story. Tell about the pictures. What are you doing in your favorite one? What are you thinking?

3. The boy was adventurous—he couldn't walk, but he rode horses. What other sport or activity do you think he might like to try? Why do you think so?

MINNIE
THE MAMBO MOSQUITO

by Carmen Tafolla
illustrated by Ruben Ramos

Minnie the Mosquito *loved* to dance!

> *She danced the mambo and the bamba,*
> *And the Cotton-eyed Joe!*
> *She danced the cumbia and the samba*
> *And the waltz just so!*
> *She danced the Mexican polka*
> *And the twist while she flew!*
> *She danced the boogie-woogie*
> *And the hokey-pokey, too!*

Minnie traveled far and wide to find music—but whenever she found it, and started dancing, someone would turn off the radio and say, "I hear mosquitoes. Let's go inside."

Or the band would stop playing and say, "There are too many bugs out here. Let's go home."

Or the choir would stop singing and say, "Let's go inside before the mosquitoes start biting."

When that happened, Minnie would buzz, "Wait a minute! I'm not like those other mosquitoes that bite! I just like to dance!" But they never heard her.

All of her mosquito friends would practice their flying stunts.

They would practice dive-bombing.

Vrrr-rrr-RRRR-RRROOM!

They would practice biting.

Ping - OUCH!

But Minnie just practiced dancing—every time she heard music.

> She danced the mambo and the bamba,
> And the Cotton-eyed Joe!
> She danced the cumbia and the samba
> And the waltz just so!
> She danced the Mexican polka
> And the twist while she flew!
> She danced the boogie-woogie
> And the hokey-pokey, too!

One day, Minnie found Fred.

Fred loved music almost as much as Minnie loved dancing. He liked to play his radio in the morning. He liked to play his radio in the afternoon. He even liked to play his radio all night long! Fred *never* turned his radio off.

Minnie liked Fred.

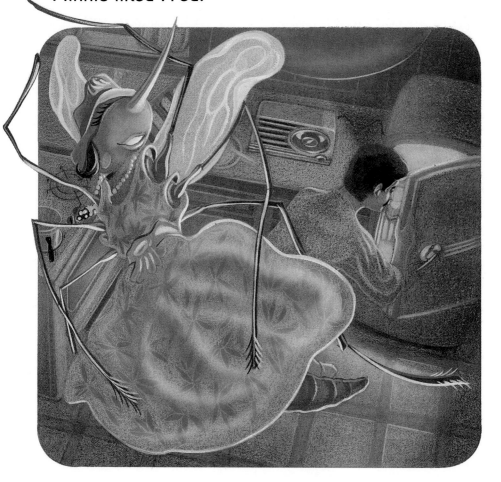

When Fred's radio played a waltz, Minnie waltzed while Fred sang "La—la—la—la la! La la! La la!" When Fred's radio played a Mexican polka, Minnie danced the Mexican polka while Fred shouted, "¡A-jai!" When Fred's radio played the Cotton-eyed Joe, Minnie danced the Cotton-eyed Joe while Fred said, "Aw-haw!"

While all the other mosquitoes were practicing their flying stunts,

and their dive-bombing,

and their biting,

Minnie just practiced her dancing.

She danced the mambo and the bamba,
And the Cotton-eyed Joe!
She danced the cumbia and the samba
And the waltz just so!
She danced the Mexican polka
And the twist while she flew!
She danced the boogie-woogie
And the hokey-pokey, too!

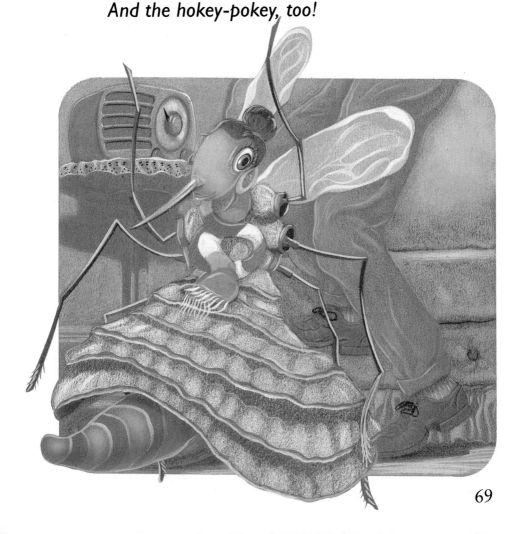

And she never bit Fred at all.

But one day, Fred turned off the radio.

Minnie couldn't believe it! For the first time in her life, she went

Whirrrrrrr → Vrrr-rrr RRRoom

Pi-

But at the very last minute, Minnie took a good look at Fred. She thought about all the good times they had together. She thought about their waltzes, and their polkas, and their Cotton-eyed Joes . . .

and Minnie flew up to Fred's ear and said, "Bz—Bz—Bz—buzz buzz! Buzz buzz! Buzz buzz!"

Something about that buzzing sound made Fred think of music again. Fred turned the radio back on.

And as for Minnie—

She danced the mambo and the bamba,
And the Cotton-eyed Joe!
She danced the cumbia and the samba
And the waltz just so!
She danced the Mexican polka
And the twist while she flew!
She danced the boogie-woogie
And the hokey-pokey, too!

THE WAY I WRITE, AND WRITE, AND WRITE

by Carmen Tafolla

When I write a story, I put my ideas down first. I write down everything I want to happen in the story, no matter how long or how short it is. It might even be just half an idea. If I am far from home when an idea comes to me, I'll write my idea down on a note pad, the back of an envelope, or a paper napkin!

Sometimes I don't know what to write next. When I first wrote *Minnie,* I was thinking about a happy little mosquito who loved to dance to every kind of music. But I didn't really know what was going to happen in the story. I just kept writing until the ideas came to me.

If I got stuck, I'd ask myself what Minnie would want in the story. In my head, I could imagine a little mosquito voice buzzing "Yezz! Yezz!" or "No, I zon't zink zzzo!"

After I write everything down for a story, I read it over to myself. If it doesn't sound right, I go back and fix it up again. I might change a word, add a sentence, or drop one.

When I write a story for children, I read it to Mari, my seven-year-old daughter. If she doesn't understand it, or if she thinks something is boring, she'll tell me. Then I work on the story again until it's the best it can be.

Mari helped me with *Minnie the Mambo Mosquito*. When I first wrote the story, Minnie bit Fred at the end. But Mari didn't like the ending. She was shocked! I realized that it wasn't a good idea to have Minnie bite Fred, so I changed the story. Do you like the new ending better?

My daughter Mari now writes her own stories. I'll bet you can too! When *you're* writing, don't forget: never be afraid to take something good and make it better.

THINKING ABOUT IT

1. Over and over, the story tells how Minnie *loved* to dance. Read about her dancing again and show how she did it.

2. Carmen Tafolla changed the ending of her story about Minnie. Did she make the right decision? Explain your answer.

3. One, two, cha-cha-cha! What do you suppose Minnie would do at a dance contest? Why do you think so?

GINO BADINO

by Diana Engel

For as long as anyone could remember, the Badino family had been making pasta—spinach pasta, egg pasta, carrot, and tomato.

The family factory was a bustling, busy place
where everyone had a special job . . . even
Gino, the youngest Badino. His job was to
sweep the factory floor each day after school.

Gino hated his job and looked for any excuse
not to do it.

One day, he picked up a nice-looking piece
of dough and squeezed it through his fingers.
"This stuff is great!" he said. "It feels like clay!"

"Don't forget your sweeping," said Mama as
she mixed just the right amount of flour and
water and eggs.

"And when you're finished," said Grandma,
testing a new recipe, "come taste this . . .
broccoli pasta!"

But Gino had other things in mind. He twisted and molded the piece of dough until he found the right shape.

In the morning, his little mouse was hard and dry. Now I'll try something a little bigger, he thought.

Each day, Gino picked up bits and pieces of discarded dough. He loved feeling the softness take shape in his hands. He made all sorts of creatures, but his favorites were the mice.

His fingers always busy, Gino watched his family work.

"I wish you'd remember to collect your little friends," said his sister, Leonora.

"Me, too!" said Uncle Dom, poring over the list of stores that sold Badino pasta.

82

Gino had trouble remembering.

But while he played, his fingers grew more sure, his ideas more wonderful.

"What's this?" cried Mama at bath time. "More dough?"

Gino was so busy, he didn't even hear.

Soon Gino's friends were treated to special birthday gifts . . . and Gino's creations were the hit of Show and Tell.

In fact, the art teacher thought Gino's work deserved a special display of its own.

But at home, the thing that Gino liked to do best only got him into trouble.

"Every day you sit there playing with dough!"
his father would shout. "Where's the broom?
Where's the dustpan? You've got work to do!"

Now, the Badinos were a kind family and
they loved their little Gino very much. But they
had to work hard to keep their business going.
They had no time for Gino's macaroni animals
and fancy shapes.

Late one night, Gino heard voices outside his
bedroom door.

"Our little business is not doing well," said
Uncle Dom. "The big companies can make
more pasta in one hour than we can make in
one day!"

"Aagh!" said Grandma. "That stuff tastes
like cardboard!"

"I know," said Mama, "but if they make more
pasta, they can sell it for less."

"Then," said Papa, "we'll make more pasta
and sell ours for less, too!"

"But how can we work harder than we do
now?" asked Uncle Dom. They all sat at the
table in gloomy silence.

Gino called out to his father. "I can help," he said. "Give me a real job, and I know I can help."

"When you are bigger, my little linguine," said Papa. "When you are bigger."

In the morning, Gino was up early. He ran downstairs to the factory.

"I'll show them I can do a real job," he muttered. "We need more pasta? I'll make more pasta!"

Grabbing bags of flour and cartons of eggs, Gino began to fill the great pasta machine.

He pushed the button and waited for the smooth, flat sheets of dough to roll out.

At first, nothing happened. Then there was a loud belching noise. There was another belch, a squeak, a huge grunt . . .

. . . and an enormous explosion!
     Like a volcano, the machine spit out a great
gush of dough, sending it so high that golden
pasta rained all over the factory floor.

To Gino, it was all quite beautiful.

The machine was quiet. He could hear his family stomping down the stairs.

Gino knew he was in big trouble.

"Gino!" shouted Papa. "What have you done?"

"What a mess!" cried Mama. "What a mess!"

"That boy had better grow up fast," said Grandma.

Uncle Dom picked up a mop. "Let's get to work," he said. "We've got to get another shipment out or we're really sunk."

The Badinos worked frantically, all day and all night.

In the confusion, a few mistakes were made.

Finally, a new shipment of pasta was ready for Uncle Dom's truck.

Gino, who hadn't touched a piece of dough since the explosion, swept quietly. Something odd in one of the boxes caught his eye.

"Oh no!" he groaned. A Gino Badino macaroni mouse stared happily from the window of the box.

Gino didn't dare say a word.

A week later, at the end of a busy day, there was a knock at the door. It was the owner of a store that sold Badino pasta.

"Is there something wrong?" asked Mama.

"I've come about those macaroni mice," he said.

Mama stared at him, bewildered.

The store owner smiled. "You know, the ones that were packed in that last shipment. There was a clown mouse and a cowboy mouse—"

"Gino!" Papa shouted. He looked like the pasta machine about to explode.

"Oh, so this is the artist," said the man.
"Great idea! Very creative! Every box is sold.
Now everyone wants to collect those little
creatures. I can sell as many as you've got!
When's the next shipment?"

Papa opened his mouth, but nothing came out.

"Right away," said Grandma quickly, "right
away!"

After the man left, Gino looked at his father. At first, nothing happened. Then Papa laughed so loud, the windows shook. Soon all the Badinos were laughing. Gino laughed longer than anyone.

"Well, son," said Papa, "you've got a big job tomorrow."

The next afternoon, Papa picked up the broom.

"You've got more important things to do than sweeping," he said. "I want to see some more of those famous macaroni mice!"

Gino was truly happy. His afternoons were
full of real work.

And his nights were full of pasta.

THINKING ABOUT IT

1. Gino's talent is making mice from pasta dough. What is your talent? Explain it. What other things would you like to do well?

2. Who ever heard of mice making macaroni, or mosquitoes dancing the mambo? Explain how the animals in the last two stories are different from real animals.

3. Oops! If the macaroni mice hadn't fallen into the pasta boxes, what could the family have done to save their business? Why do you think so?

Another Book of Animal Fantasy
In *Three Cheers for Errol* by Babette Cole, Errol the rat must use his brain when he competes in the Ratathalon.

by James Stevenson

It was very cold on the iceberg.

"It's too cold to sit around," said Ralph.

"It's too cold to go swimming," said Alf.

"Let's go for a walk," said Merrill.

"Good idea," said Darryl.

The ice was as slippery as glass.

It was hard to walk without falling down.

Ralph and Alf and Merrill and Darryl
held onto each other.
"Oh-oh," said Darryl.
"Here comes Cheryl!"

"You'll crash into us!" said Merrill.

"Stop!" said Darryl.

"Stop!" said Alf.

"How?" said Cheryl.

Cheryl crashed into Darryl.

Darryl crashed into Merrill.

Merrill crashed into Alf.

Alf crashed into Ralph.

"Hey!" said Ralph.

"Where are you going, Ralph?" called Alf.

"I have no idea," called Ralph.

"Be careful," called Darryl.

"Thanks," said Ralph.

"Try to turn, Ralph!" called Alf.

"I'm trying," called Ralph.

"Ralph's turning," said Alf.
"Now he's coming back," said Merrill.
"Look out!" said Darryl.
"Stop, Ralph!" called Alf.

"I'm back," said Ralph.
"We know," said Alf.

"Oh-oh," said Cheryl.

"What now?" said Darryl.

"Here comes Beryl," said Cheryl.

"Maybe she'll miss us," said Darryl.

"I hope so," said Cheryl.

"Somebody grab my wing!" said Beryl.

"Not me!" said Cheryl.

"Or me!" said Darryl.

"Here!" said Ralph. "I'll help you."
"Oh-oh!" said everybody.

They flew across the ice.
At last they began to slow down.
But the end of the iceberg was just ahead.

They came to a stop at the very
edge of the ice.

"That was close," said Ralph.

"We almost fell in," said Alf.

"And it looks awfully cold."

"Where's Beryl?" said Cheryl.

"Here I am!" said Beryl.

"Sorry," said Beryl. "It was slippery."
"We know," said Darryl.
"It's not so cold," said Cheryl.
"Once you get in," said the others.
"That's what I mean," said Cheryl,
  and they all went for a swim.

THINKING ABOUT IT

1. How would you show someone what happened to Ralph, Alf, Merrill, Darryl, Cheryl, and Beryl? Did anything like this ever happen to you? Explain.

2. Are penguins easy to draw? How does James Stevenson make them look like they're moving? Explain.

3. Sit-ups! Jumping jacks! Headstands! What might happen if the six penguins visit your gym class? Why?

More Stories by James Stevenson
Oh No, It's Waylon's Birthday! is filled with silly stories about animals.

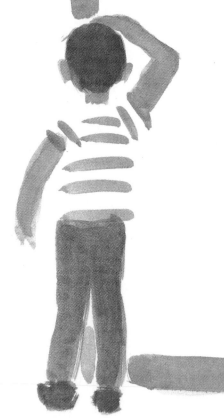

Higher
on the
Door

by James Stevenson

*I have a grandson now; that's how old I am. But
sometimes I look back and remember...*

Years ago, on our birthdays, our mother
marked on a doorway how much we
had grown.

THE YEAR
THAT MY
BROTHER WAS
THIS TALL

I WAS THIS TALL

AND OUR DOG JOCKO WAS THIS TALL

We lived on a street in a village by the river.

CLINK
CLINK

DRIP
DRIP

On our street, the milkman brought milk in glass bottles, and took away the empties.

The iceman brought ice for our icebox,

and the coal truck came and sent coal thundering into our cellar.

We knew our neighbors pretty well.

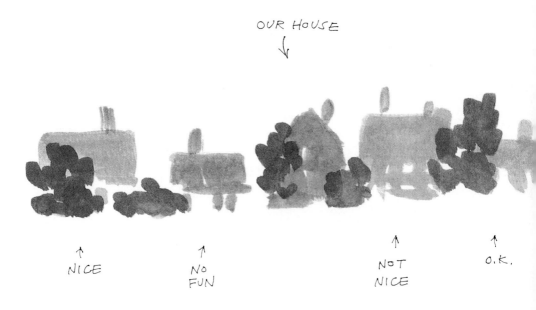

OUR HOUSE

NICE

NO
FUN

NOT
NICE

O.K.

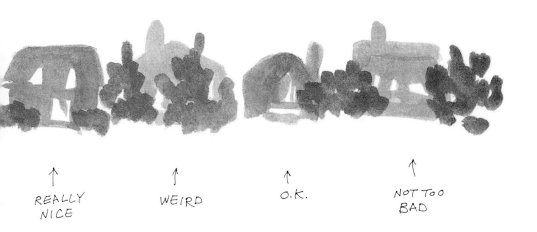

REALLY
NICE

WEIRD

O.K.

NOT TOO
BAD

115

On the wall of the post office in the village were pictures of criminals nobody could find. There was a big reward if you found them, so . . . my brother and I kept our eye out.

There were a lot of things I couldn't do.

I couldn't make a loud whistle with two fingers. I couldn't learn to juggle. But I could wiggle my ears one at a time.

And I could fall over on my face without getting hurt. (You put your hands up at the very last minute.)

Across the street were woods.
In the summer there were vines to swing on.

In the winter we built forts and threw
snowballs. We made tunnels in the snow.

If it wasn't snowing or raining, my brother and
I walked to school. Jocko watched us.

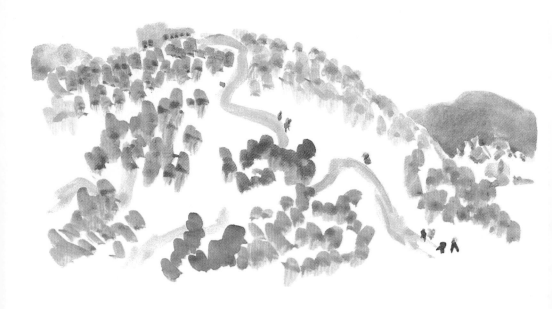

The village had steep hills and twisty roads.
Other children joined us on the way to school.

I liked making things
with clay in art class.

You took a fat hunk
of it

and rolled it into a
long piece

and curled it around

and put it on top of
another long, curled
piece, and another.

Then you smoothed
it all out and painted
it and baked it—

and took it home to your mother.

IT'S FOR
YOU.

OH, HOW
LOVELY!

Sometimes it was hard for me to pay attention
in school.

What was on the blackboard was never as interesting as what was out the window.

And Davey Gronowski was always making me laugh.

My brother liked to scare me.

He said I was a scaredy-cat and afraid of everything. That wasn't true. . . .

The only things I was afraid of were:

BEES

HOSPITALS

BATS

THE DENTIST

SNAKES

TOUGH KIDS

IODINE ON CUTS

TICKS ON JOCKO

THE BULL THAT
LIVED IN THE
MEADOW DOWN
THE ROAD

LIGHTNING

THE DARK

I was also afraid of the dam breaking.
Sometimes we went for a picnic at a big dam.
My brother would suddenly say, "I think the
dam is breaking," and I would start to run.

The worst thing that happened was when
Jocko got hit by a car. No bones were broken,
but he was hurt.

HERE'S SOME
WATER, JOCKO

HERE'S A BONE

Jocko stayed very quiet for a few days and
then he got well again.

My brother kept a diary. He wrote in it every
day. I begged him to let me see it.

One day, when he was away, I took his diary
down from the shelf . . . and I read it.

Every day was the same!
I put it back on the shelf.

Sometimes our family would take the train to New York City. The railroad station was at the edge of the river. You had to go over an overpass to get to the track.

While you were waiting, you could watch fast trains coming with thick smoke and cinders flying from their smokestacks. At the last minute . . . you'd run for safety!

When the train for New York arrived, we'd climb aboard.

My father was used to going on the train, so he read the newspaper. The seats were shiny woven wicker. If it was hot, you could open the window and get the breeze.

There was plenty to see.

In New York we once went to the top of the
Empire State Building.

We always had lunch at the Automat. The food was behind small glass windows. When you saw just what you wanted, you put money in a slot, turned a knob, opened the window, and took it out.

The most exciting time in New York was when we went to see our grandparents sail away on a big ocean liner. A band played, and everybody waved and threw confetti.

When the ship's whistle blew, the whole city seemed to shake.

Tugboats pushed the ocean liner down the river toward the sea.

I wished I could go.

On the way home I asked, "Can I go on an ocean liner?"

"When you get older," my parents said. . . .

I couldn't wait to get higher on the door.

Jim Davis and Me

by James Stevenson

I didn't read a real book—one that wasn't mostly pictures, I mean—until I was ten. Before that, I read comic books and the Johnson-Smith catalog, which offered thrilling items you could send away for. There were things like a periscope for spying around corners and over fences, a disguise kit that would make you unrecognizable even to your own parents, and a device that would allow you to "throw your voice" and make people think somebody was trapped inside a cupboard. ("Help! Let me out!")

But the items I sent for never quite worked. The periscope fell apart in the rain. The disguise fooled nobody. When I tried to surprise my friends by voice-throwing, they asked why I was talking in that strangled voice with my teeth clenched.

When I was ten, things changed. Our teacher announced that from now on we would each take one book out of the school library every week and actually read it. We all felt this was unreasonable, but we went along, grumbling. I found a book called *Jim Davis* by John Masefield, and picked it because the hero and I shared the same first name. Jim's life was a lot more exciting than mine, full of ships, swords, horses, dark nights, and pirates, and I liked the book so much I took it out of the library every week.

When, after some months, the librarian refused to let me renew *Jim Davis* again, I was forced to look for something else. I was not optimistic, but gradually I discovered that books—unlike the Johnson-Smith catalog—sometimes kept their promises. In their pages you could see around corners and over fences, you could hear voices, and you could become somebody else. That's when I began to read.

PULLING THE THEME TOGETHER
SUCCESS!

1. James Stevenson couldn't wait to get "higher on the door." What do you look forward to doing when you get older? Why?

2. Find two of your favorite parts in this book. Practice telling them to someone else. Get ready for a festival. In the festival you will present your favorite two things from this book.

3. Give an award to Sam or Nessa or Gino. What will the award be? Why? What will they say when they receive it?

135

BOOKS TO ENJOY

The Wednesday Surprise

by Eve Bunting
Illustrations by Donald Carrick
Grandma and Anna are planning
a surprise for Dad's birthday.
Who will really be surprised?

The Cow Buzzed

by Andrea Zimmerman and David Clemesha
Illustrations by Paul Meisel

A smart rabbit tries to give
advice to the farm animals.
When they don't listen, the
farm becomes a very funny
and mixed-up place!

We Can't Sleep

Written and illustrated by James Stevenson
It's too hot for Louie and Mary Ann to sleep,
so Grandpa entertains them with some of his
wild stories.

A Picture Book of Helen Keller

by David A. Adler

Helen Keller is blind and deaf, and no one thinks she can learn anything. She acts so wild that her teacher almost gives up. But in this true story, Helen surprises everyone.

Snowy

by Berlie Doherty

Illustrations by Keith Bowen

When Rachel's classmates bring their pets to school, she feels left out because she can't bring in the horse that pulls her barge home.

Galimoto

by Karen Lynn Williams

Illustrations by Catherine Stock

What is a galimoto? Seven-year-old Kondi knows, and he looks all around his African village to find everything he needs to make one.

LITERARY TERMS

Animal Fantasy

An **animal fantasy** is a make-believe story about animals that act like people. *Minnie the Mambo Mosquito* is an animal fantasy.

Autobiography

In an **autobiography** you tell about yourself. In *Higher on the Door,* James Stevenson tells about things that happened when he was growing up. If you wrote your autobiography, what would you tell?

Poetry

Some **poetry** rhymes, like "To Catch a Fish" on page 46. Some poems do not rhyme, like *With the Wind* on pages 48–62. Poems can be written in many different ways.

Realistic Fiction

A story that could really happen is **realistic fiction.** Both *Soccer Sam* and *Nessa's Fish* are realistic fiction. The characters seem like real people.

Setting

The **setting** is when and where a story happens. In some stories, the setting causes the problems for the characters in the story. In *Nessa's Fish* the setting is the tundra. The wild animals that live on the tundra create problems that Nessa must solve.

GLOSSARY

Words from your stories

a•mong   in the group of: *Divide the fruit among all of us.*

cel•lar   a space under a building or house, usually used to store food: *We keep potatoes in the cellar.* **cellars.**

coal   a black rock that gives off heat when it is burned: *Coal comes from plants that died millions of years ago.* **coals.**

coal

crea•ture   any person or animal: *We took in the lost dog because the poor creature was homeless.* **creatures.**

crim•i•nal   a person who has committed a crime: *The police chased the criminal.* **criminals.**

dam   a wall built to hold back the water of a creek or river: *Beavers built a dam in the stream.* **dams.**

dash   to rush: *We dashed down the street to catch the bus.* **dashed, dashing.**

dash

di•ar•y a written record of what one does or thinks each day: *Reggie always writes in his diary.* **diaries.**

dis•card to throw away; give up as useless or worn out: *Angie discarded her old clothing.* **discarded, discarding.**

dive-bomb to attack while swooping down: *The mother bird dive-bombed the hungry cat.* **dive-bombed, dive-bombing.**

dough a soft, thick mixture of flour and other things used to make bread, cake, pasta, and so on: *This dough needs more water.* **doughs.**

drib•ble to move a ball by bouncing it or giving it short kicks: *Sandra dribbled the basketball down the court.* **dribbled, dribbling.**

diary

dribble

edge the line or place where something ends: *He parked at the edge of the road.* **edges.**

ex•plo•sion a blowing up; bursting with a loud noise: *The car crash caused an explosion.* **explosions.**

free•dom The condition of being free; not under someone else's control: *The people hoped to find freedom in a new land.* **freedoms.**

hoof

hoof   the hard part of the foot of some animals: *Horses, cattle, sheep, and pigs have hoofs on their feet.* **hoofs, hooves.**

hooves   See **hoof.**

ice·berg   a large piece of ice floating in the sea: *The seals played on the iceberg.* **icebergs.**

iceberg

in·land   away from the seacoast or the border: *The seagulls flew inland to escape the storm.*

in·tro·duce   to tell people each other's names when they don't know each other: *I introduced my mom to my new friend Pat.* **introduced, introducing.**

lope   to run with a long, easy stride: *The wolves loped along the shore of the lake.* **loped, loping.**

mac·a·ro·ni   a food made of flour and water, dried in the shape of hollow tubes: *Should we have macaroni or spaghetti for supper?*

mold   to form into a shape: *We molded the dough into loaves to be baked.* **molded, molding.**

mo·squi·to   a small insect that bites people and animals and causes itching: *The mosquitoes are biting tonight.* **mosquitoes,** *or* **mosquitos.**

mosquito

prac·tice   to do something again and again so you learn to do it well: *Sonji practiced her flute every day.* **practiced, practicing.**

ra·di·o   an electric machine that brings voices and music from far away: *We listened to the game on the car radio.* **radios.**

radio

shiv·er   to shake with cold or fear: *I shivered in the cold wind.* **shivered, shivering.**

shuf·fle   to scrape or drag the feet while walking: *It's hard not to shuffle when you wear slippers.* **shuffled, shuffling.**

slip·per·y   causing one to slide or fall: *The icy sidewalk is slippery.* **slipperier, slipperiest.**

slippery

strength   the condition of being strong; power; force: *She had the strength to move the stone.*

strength·en   to make stronger; to grow stronger: *Exercise will strengthen your body.* **strengthened, strengthening.**

ACKNOWLEDGMENTS

Text
Page 6: *Soccer Sam* by Jean Marzollo. Text copyright © 1987 by Jean Marzollo. Reprinted by permission of Random House, Inc.
Page 28: From *Nessa's Fish* by Nancy Luenn, illustrated by Neil Waldman. Copyright © 1990 by Nancy Luenn. Illustrations copyright © 1990 by Neil Waldman. Reprinted by permission of Atheneum Publishers, an imprint of Macmillan Publishing Company.
Page 46: "To Catch a Fish" from *Under the Sunday Tree* by Eloise Greenfield. Illustrated by Mr. Amos Ferguson. Paintings copyright © 1988 by Amos Ferguson. Text copyright © 1988 by Eloise Greenfield. Reprinted by permission of HarperCollins Publishers.
Page 48: *With the Wind* by Liz Damrell, pictures by Stephen Marchesi. Text copyright © 1991 by Liz Damrell. Illustrations copyright © 1991 by Stephen Marchesi. All rights reserved. Reprinted by permission of Orchard Books, New York.
Page 64: "Minnie the Mambo Mosquito," by Carmen Tafolla. Copyright © by Carmen Tafolla, 1991.
Page 72: "The Way I Write, and Write, and Write," by Carmen Tafolla. Copyright © by Carmen Tafolla, 1991.
Page 76: *Gino Badino* by Diana Engel. Copyright © 1991 by Diana Engel. Published by Morrow Junior Books. Reprinted by permission of William Morrow and Company, Inc. Publishers.
Page 98: "Slippery Ice" from *Oh No, It's Waylon's Birthday!* by James Stevenson. Copyright © 1989 by James Stevenson. Published by Greenwillow Books, a Division of William Morrow & Company, Inc. Reprinted by permission of William Morrow and Company, Inc. Publishers.

Page 110: *Higher on the Door* by James Stevenson. Copyright © 1987 by James Stevenson. Published by Greenwillow Books, a Division of William Morrow & Company, Inc. Reprinted by permission of William Morrow and Company, Inc.
Page 132: "Jim Davis and Me," by James Stevenson. Copyright © by James Stevenson, 1991.

Artists
Illustrations owned and copyrighted by the illustrator.
David McPhail, cover, 1–5, 135–144
Chris Hopkins, 6–27
Neil Waldman, 28–45
Amos Ferguson, 47
Stephen Marchesi, 48–63
Ruben Ramos, 64–75
Diana Engel, 76–97
James Stevenson, 98–131

Photographs
Unless otherwise acknowledged, all photographs are the property of Scott Foresman.
Page 72: Courtesy of Carmen Tafolla
Page 132: Photo by Edwina Stevenson

Glossary
The contents of this glossary have been adapted from *My Second Picture Dictionary*, Copyright © 1990 Scott, Foresman and Company and *Beginning Dictionary*, Copyright © 1988 Scott, Foresman and Company.